AF429014

Hex codes, or hexadecimal codes, are a way to represent colors in digital devices and web design. Each hex code refers to a very specific color. A hex color is expressed as a six-digit combination of numbers and letters, preceded by a pound sign or hashtag, defined by its mix of red, green, and blue (RGB). The first two letters or numbers refer to red, the next two refer to green, and the last two refer to blue.

The color values are defined as values between 00 and FF. Hex codes are a universal way to describe colors. This book is specifically about shades of purple.

A is for affair purple

A

#73488D

a is for african violet

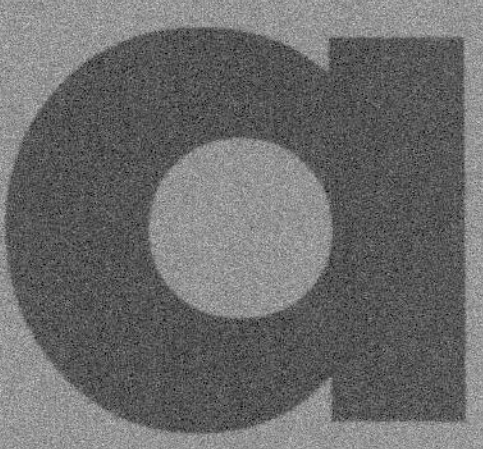

#B284BE

B is for biloba flower

B

#B2A1EA

b is for butterfly bush

b

#624E9A

C is for clairvoyant

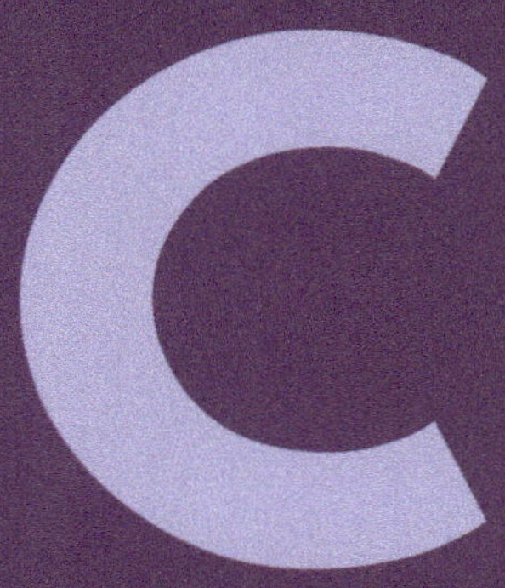

#480656

c is for cold purple

C

#ABA0D9

D is for deluge

D

#7563AB

d is for dioxazine
purple

d

#422A79

E is for east side

E

#AC91CE

e is for electric lavender

e

#F4BBFF

F is for ferris wheel

F

#724AA1

f is for fog

f

#D7D0FF

G is for genie purple

#933E77

g is for giggle

g

#69326E

H is for highlight
H
#333a39

h is for honey flower

#4HC70

J is for japanese violet

J

#5B3256

j is for jelly

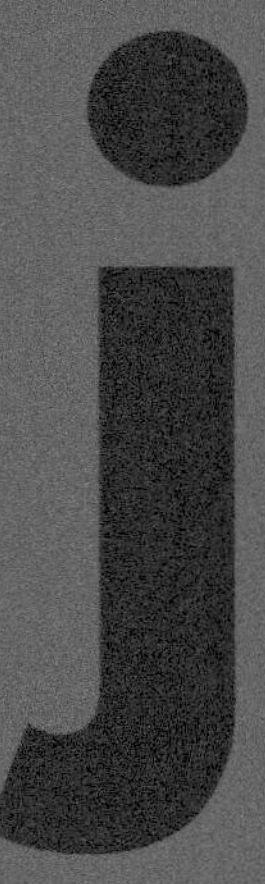

#A02OF0

K is for kaleidoscope

K

#3A084F

k is for kingfisher purple

k

#583580

L is for lipstick stain

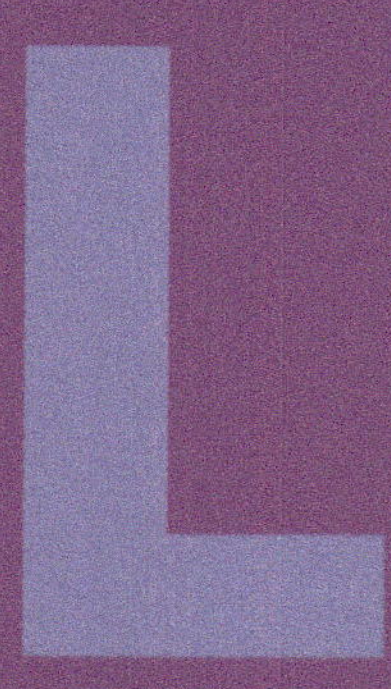

#8E4785

l is for long shot

l

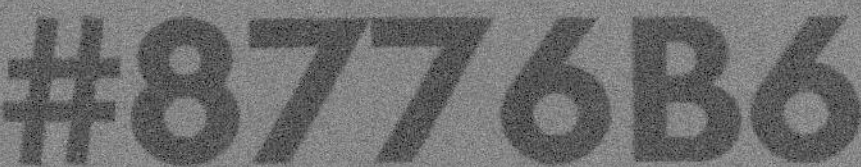
#8776B6

M is for mardi gras

M

#880085

m is for midnight pearl

m

#702670

N is for navy purple

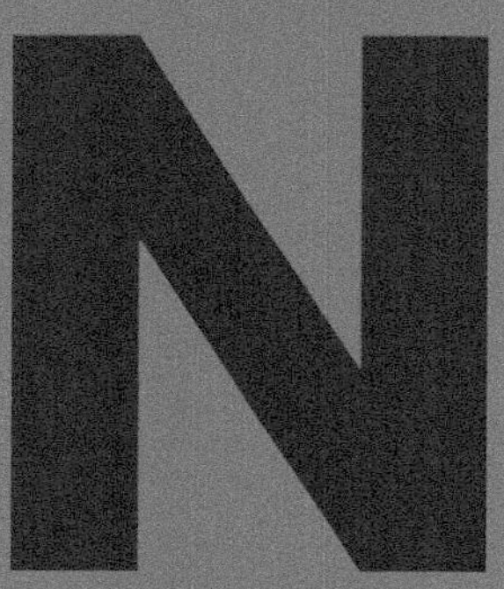

#9457EB

n is for nightclub

n

#6A1F44

O is for ooh la la
#AOBBA6

o is for opera mauve

#B784A7

P is for pearly purple

P

#B768A2

p is for purpureus

#9A4EAE

Q is for queenly

#D3ABCD

q is for quinacridone
red violet

q

#740055

R is for razzmic berry

R

#8D4E85

r is for regalia

r

#522D80

S is for sassy

S

#7E2A65

s is for sweet purple

s

#8953DC

T is for tropical violet

T

#CDA4DE

t is for true v

t

#8A73D6

U is for unicorn

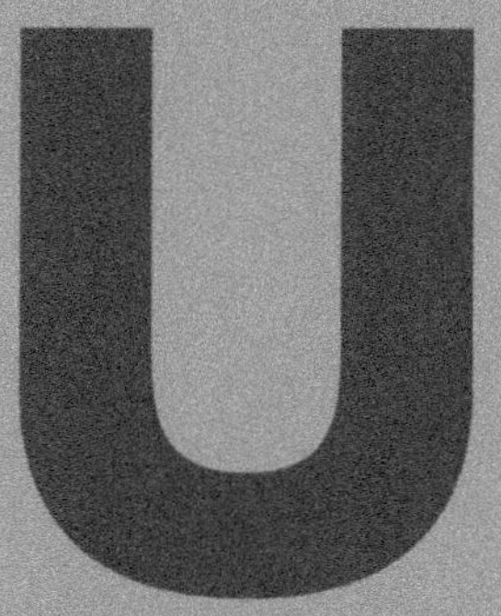

#9F90D0

u is for urban purple

U

#503F76

V is for velvet mauve

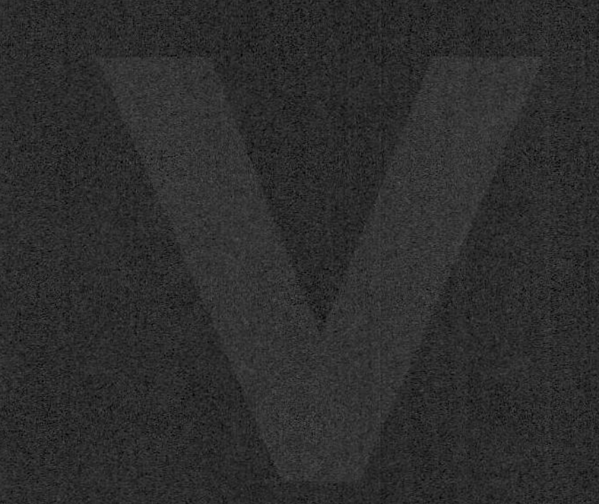

#692B57

v is for violet

#732E6C

W is for windsor

W

#3C0878

w is for wonderland

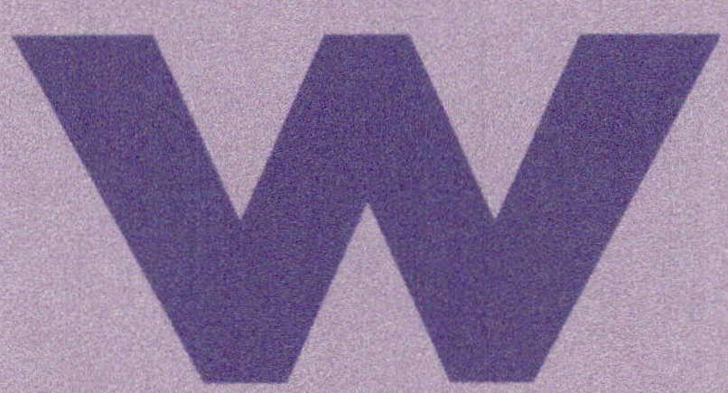

#BB97BB

X is for xi hu huanghun

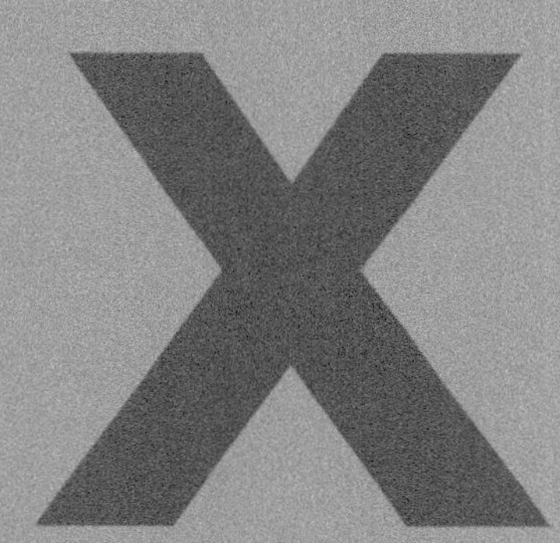

#A095B0

x is for xoxo

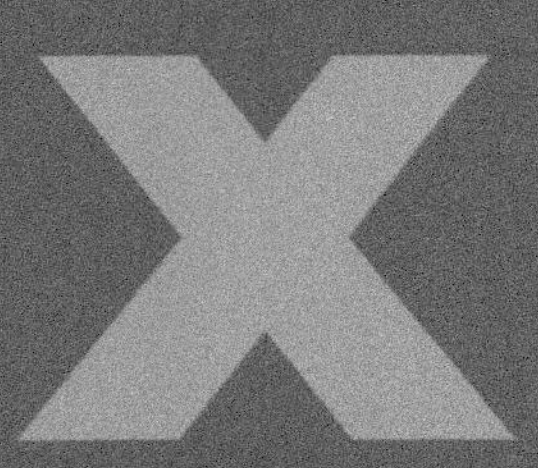

#904F7D

Y is for yen magenta

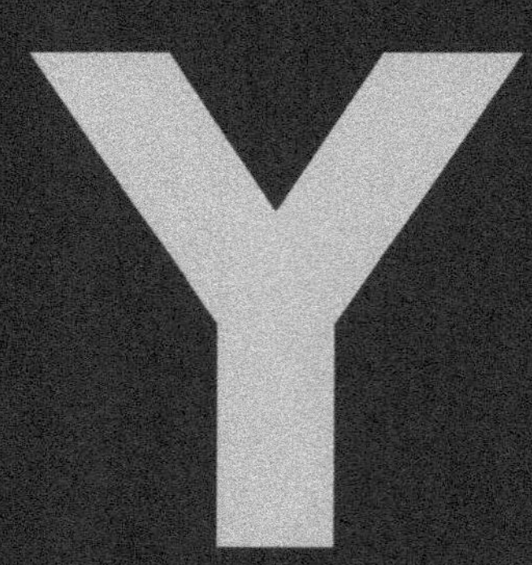

#330033

y is for yesterday's roses

y

#DOBCC3